It's All About the Shoes

HOPE, HEARTBREAK AND
THE SEARCH FOR THE PERFECT PAIR

*Wear your own shoes and
enjoy your life's journey.*

Yvonne L. Williams

6/22/07

Yvonne L. Williams

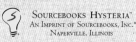

SOURCEBOOKS HYSTERIA™
AN IMPRINT OF SOURCEBOOKS, INC.®
NAPERVILLE, ILLINOIS

Published by Sourcebooks, Inc.

P.O. Box 4410, Naperville, Illinois 60567-4410

(630) 961-3900

Fax: (630) 961-2168

www.sourcebooks.com

ISBN-13: 978-1-4022-0712-9

ISBN-10: 1-4022-0712-3

Printed and bound in China

IM 10 9 8 7 6 5 4 3 2 1

To my daughter Danielle

Acknowledgments

To all those who contributed to this book:
I could not have done it without you; may you
be showered with blessings.
Special thanks to: William, Robert, Beth, Chalene,
Danielle, Debbie, Elizabeth, Jane, Lindsay, Molly,
Onawumi, Phyllis, and Vickie, and
at Sourcebooks: Deb, Rebecca, Susie, and Anne.
And to Whitney, Jennifer, and Tara,
thanks for the use of your shoes.

A day in tight shoes is still a good day.

Contents

Introduction

Shoes Stories from Women's Soles to Women's Souls

*I*nspiration can come from the most unlikely places. Need we look only to our feet to find it? That's what I started to wonder after my chance encounter with a roomful of passionate shoe talkers. As I traveled around the country for my speaking engagements, I started to ask women everywhere to share their shoe memories and mishaps. And the more tales I collected, the more I came to believe there is a sole-soul connection. That is, the stories of women and their shoes provide humor to lighten the day, encouragement to keep us going, or even nuggets of wisdom for living more meaningful lives.

Like most women, I love my shoes. The number of pairs I own puzzles my husband, and from what he says, many men share his perplexity.

"I can understand you owning a few pairs, but why so many shoes, why the obsession?" he asked with genuine curiosity.

My reply is simple: "Women see in color, men in black and white."

But there's really no one answer. It's about ownership, about defining who you are, about the hunt, the excitement, the rush of acquiring. It's about showing off to your girlfriends, feeling sexy, walking tall, looking good, and feeling good. It's about style and color, highs and lows—heels and flats—about choice and change and satisfying oneself. It's also about being comfortable with one's femininity and sexuality; it's about color, beauty, and touch.

For me, like many women, footwear goes far beyond covering my feet. Our shoes transform us. Just think about how your deportment changes when you slip on a new pair of sleek heels or a comfy pair of pink sneakers. Shoes are a way to express ourselves and to be unique. And ultimately, shoes are about love—the more you have, the more you want—and with the average women owning over thirty pairs, women simply can't get enough.

In our passion for shoes, however, women can sometimes forget that the purpose of our footwear is to protect us from the elements and shield us from dangerous ground. We sometimes fail to consider comfort, longevity, or whether our shoes are the right ones for the journey. And instead of pleasant memories from an enjoyable walk, we can be left with pinches, aches, scars, and distortions. Likewise, when we fail to carefully break in situations before getting involved, we end up with blisters on our souls—much like the ones on our soles.

Most women have more shoes than they need, can afford, or have room to store. And in the rest of our lives, we also take on more than we can reasonably handle. As life becomes cluttered with shoes that never should have been bought and commitments that never should have been made, we experience an increasing loss of control over our space and our lives.

With so many shoes to take care of, sometimes it becomes hard to find the time to properly maintain them. And just as with shoes, in my own life I allowed myself to become beat up and rundown from not taking care of myself—emotions and self-esteem scuffed and worn. My shoes needed new heels to elevate me. But it took a nearly fatal three-prong cancer diagnosis to motivate me to make the necessary repairs that would ultimately heal my soul.

Yes, like most women, I have bought shoes that are a size too small or the wrong ones for the situation. But now I know there's no substitute for a pair that slips on easily, feels like heaven, looks fashionable, and can be worn for hours without causing pain. The tales in this book run the gamut from favorite pairs to nightmare pairs, heartbreak soles to heaven-sent heels, shoes that got in the way to shoes that got away! Humorous, heroic, heartwarming, heart wrenching, ordinary, and extraordinary; here are the best of the best I've collected throughout the years.

Ask any woman if she has a shoe story to tell, and you're likely to get a shoeful! Sometimes funny, sometimes touching, and sometimes profound, our stories portray the diversity of women's lives and experiences—our joys, milestones, challenges, and disappointments. And in them we find humor, wisdom, and ultimately, ourselves.

Are These Tight Enough For You?

Recently my girlfriends and I were hanging out at one of our favorite restaurants and, of course, our conversation drifted to shoe talk—which of us owned the tightest pair of shoes? It was not surprising that we all had tight shoe stories. I shared that I owned a pair of tan, stylish platform shoes that I purchased from Leeds Shoes in Los Angeles during the '70s. I can feel the pain of the hard leather even to this day. They slipped on easily, but every time I wore those shoes, I ended up wincing when I walked and got blisters on my feet. Band-Aids at the back of my heels and toes did nothing to ease the pain. I would promise God and myself that I would never wear those shoes again. I would actually go through the ritual of setting them out to throw them away, then returning them to my closet, only to wear them again. I knew that they would never change and would always cause me pain. But not only did they look good on my feet, they made me feel good when I put them on.

In every woman's closet you'll find shoes that look good but cannot be worn, shoes that cause pain or have long out-lived their usefulness. In our hearts we try to hold on to things or relationships we have outgrown, or that were never right for us in the first place. Sometimes a situation, or a person, has taught us all it can, but we have a hard time letting go.

—Y. Andrews, Los Angeles, California

Love yourself enough to let go!

Heart and Sole

Several years ago, while working at Neiman Marcus in Chicago, a young man noticed that women often left their used shoes in the shoe department after purchasing new ones. Many of them, he observed, were still in very serviceable condition. He asked the management if he could collect the discarded shoes and donate them to charity. The answer was yes, and the Saving Soles Foundation was established in Chicago. Subsequently, the Saving Soles Foundation collaborated with the Windy City Chapter of The Links, Incorporated, and Veranda Dickens, then president of the chapter. They secured over five hundred pairs of brand new shoes that were taken by the members to South Africa and given to children at the schools that The Links, Incorporated, has built in the townships. Because of this young man's ingenuity, thousands of shoes have been donated to needy people throughout the world.

—A. Dodd, Chicago, Illinois

We receive the most by giving to others.

Cash, Charge, or Heels?

After a night of partying in Manhattan, I hailed a cab. It swerved to the sidewalk and the headlights shone on my sexy black heels that had cost me a week's salary. I opened the cab door, slipped in, and was pleased to see a female driver. Upon arrival at my destination in Brooklyn, I reached into my tiny pocketbook for money to pay the fare. But there was no money, not even a penny! I pleadingly explained to the driver that I had forgotten to go to the ATM. She immediately locked the cab doors, turned around, and gave me a look that said "don't even try this with me." "I'll take your shoes instead," she said calmly, without a moment's hesitation. In a daze, I quickly removed my treasured shoes and handed them over. She unlocked the doors, I got out, and then she drove away without another word.

—C. Fife, Brooklyn, New York

Do not possess that which you are unwilling to give up.

Sometimes a Shoe Wears You

I was a diva-in-training from an early age. I hovered around my mother while she dressed meticulously . . . taking time with her makeup and hair, and carefully selecting her clothes and shoes. Oh, her shoes! Those exquisite shoes! She had the most glamorous, sexy, and colorful shoes I ever saw. It is my love for shoes and the acquisition of them that helped me walk into shoe-diva status. And it was with my conscious "shoe ranking" that I bought these drop-dead boots with the murderous four-inch stiletto heels: they were purple tweed and leather, rose to mid-calf, and were adorned with a beautiful purple brooch that gathered a strip of purple leather to the side of my ankle.

The first and only time I wore these boots was to work. Everyone who got a glimpse wanted to see more. I spent the day lifting my foot and pulling up my pant leg so everyone could admire my boots and see how stunning and tall they were. The whole office was buzzing, "Did you see Sarah's boots?" I was glad to get home and take off those boots that

had tightened with the length of day. To my surprise, I found that not only did my feet ache, but my back was in agony. I didn't know if it was from lifting my leg the whole day or from the four-inch stiletto heels. It turned out I had to remain in bed and was unable to go to work for days. My doctor later delivered the news: the boots were out. In fact, heels over two inches were out! I had a slipped disc and tall heels were a contributing factor.

For a while I still tried to wear those boots—not wanting to lose my shoe-diva status—but my back protested...and now the boots sit in their box, with me hoping that one day I may wear them again.

—S. Maloney-Yee, So. Hadley, Massachusetts

No one can take care of you...
better than you.

The Price of Exposing Your Sole

I was sitting in the waiting area of an exclusive restaurant, waiting for my friend to arrive, when a beautiful woman walked in. All eyes were on her. She was tall and aloof, about five-foot-nine, blonde, and covered in an ankle-length, honey-colored fur coat. Dripping with diamonds, she smiled only at those she knew and coldly ignored the greetings of others. Her air of superiority was just as visible as the fur coat. Before sitting down across from me, she removed her wrap to reveal a stunning three-piece outfit in various shades of brown. The dark boots she wore complemented the ensemble. I admitted to the person sitting next to me that she was certainly well put-together. Then, knowing her audience was mesmerized, the sultry blonde ceremoniously crossed her legs. My eyes were immediately drawn to something bright red that was stuck on the bottom of the sole of her right boot. I scanned the room and could see that everyone else was staring at the same spot. Upon closer scrutiny, I realized that we were all looking at a Marshall's store sale sticker showing a price of $16.99!

—B. Coulibaly, Racine, Wisconsin

It's all in the details.

Finding Your Footing

I was riding the crowded New York subway one morning to my job in midtown Manhattan when I felt a hand squeeze my bum. I turned around and the passenger behind me winked and smiled. Without hesitation, I ground my three-inch heel into his foot with all the pressure I could muster. Then I winked back at him.

—M. Symes, East Windsor, Connecticut

What you plant, you'll reap.

Using Shoes to Attract or Repel

*I*f there's one thing I've learned traveling along this life's highways and byways, it's that in all things, it is best to completely be yourself. I was thinking about this as I drove to a speaking engagement for the Los Angeles Chapter of the National Association of Women Business Owners. I was dressed in my usual give-a-speech costume—blouse, blazer, pants, and gold tennis shoes. Mind you, I wear gold tennis shoes all the time. They've become part of my brand. I've been recognized in bookstores because of my shoes! I have casual gold tennies with a quilted pattern for everyday wear, and beaded gold tennis shoes for black-tie events, but for speeches I wear dressy gold tennis shoes studded with rhinestones. I had thought briefly of wearing *real* shoes to this event, since it was at a rather corporate suity-type club, but I decided to stick with my usual style.

My momentary hesitation manifested itself in a challenge issued to me by an employee in the lobby. "Excuse me, miss," he said, frowning disapprovingly at my feet, "but we don't allow tennis shoes in our club."

Oh, dear, I thought, am I going to be thrown out? Barred from the club? I said, "You know, I'm sure your dress code means tennis shoes as in gym shoes. These are clearly not dirty, old gym shoes—they are gold mesh, dressy shoes with diamonds on them!"

He paused for a long moment as he thought this over, examining my feet. Finally he said, "Okay . . . but hurry!" He wanted me out of his jurisdiction as soon as possible, and I was happy to oblige him as I scurried upstairs to the meeting room.

The reactions to my gold shoes are always very interesting. Lots of people smile and comment how they just love my shoes, how comfortable they look, etc. I know these are My People. And of course, some people don't like them—one woman told me after a talk that I should dress more professionally if I were going to address a serious subject like money. I just smiled, because that's one of the problems I'm trying to solve—that people are too serious about money.

When you are truly yourself, other people will see it and know you for who you are. This simplifies life immeasurably. Your People will be drawn to you more quickly, and Not Your People run away far and fast. This is a good thing. You don't want your life cluttered up with a bunch of people who don't really like you. It's too much of a time and energy drain.

—*C. Campbell, author, The Wealthy Spirit
and Zero to Zillionaire*

*People—like shoes—
come in different styles.*

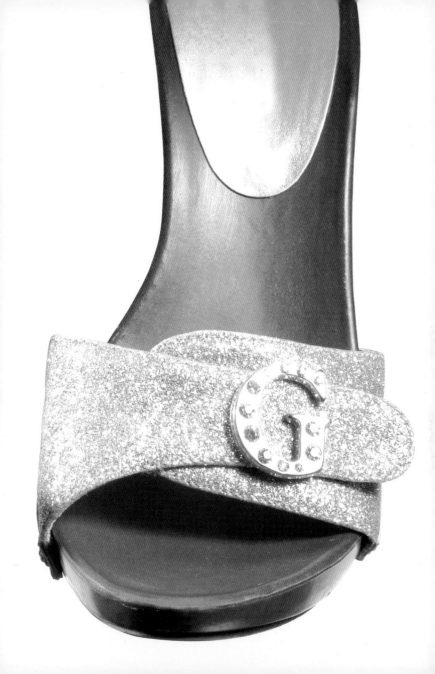

Toe to Toe

My girlfriend and I treated our teenage daughters to a luxurious Caribbean cruise. One night after dinner my daughter and I went to our rooms to change while my friend and her daughter waited for us in the nightclub. They amused themselves watching a well-dressed man on the dance floor. They suspected by the way he moved and held his head that he was a trained dancer. His shoes gave him away . . . black patent leather that shone in the dark.

He moved from woman to woman, bowing elegantly and asking them to dance. Enchanted, they gleefully accepted —only to be undone. Unable to keep up with him, many women tripped over his feet and were noticeably embarrassed. Finally he approached my friend and, with outstretched hand and a bow, asked her to join him on the dance floor. She knew she was no match for him and was not going to be another dance casualty! *Two can play this game,* she thought as she graciously declined. As soon as he moved on, she called me and gave me the rundown. I put on my dancing shoes and quickly headed to the nightclub. You see, I used to be a professional dancer and my husband and I are involved with one of the largest ballroom dance studio franchises in the country.

I entered the club and as expected, Mr. Debonair parted the sea of people to get to me. He went through his protocol of bowing and with outstretched hand asked me to dance. I accepted his invitation with a sultry tone and an ingratiating smile. Unsuspecting, he drew me close to him as he had with the others—a posture that makes dance mistakes more obvious. I was malleable in his arms . . . ready to be led. His grin broadened. We waltzed. I followed his lead so closely that he was caught off guard. He missed his steps and looked a little befuddled, while I was flawless and moved with grace. He released me, moving slightly away.

"Who are you? How do you dance so well? Where did you learn to dance?"

I smiled, pointed in the direction of my feet, and said, "It's my shoes . . . they're made for dancing."

—B. Rothweiler, Longmeadow, Massachusetts

Examine your motives before engaging.

Bare Soles

My husband was an executive with a Fortune 500™ company and we had relocated to several states during a short period, each transfer bringing with it promotional opportunities. Once again, the call to transfer came and we answered compliantly. Well versed in the rituals of moving, our house was ready and on the market in no time. During the realtors' walk-through, my six-year-old son opened my shoe closet and one hundred or so pairs of shoes that had been thrown, shoved, stacked, and tucked came tumbling out onto the floor. (I had warned him not to open the door to my shoe closet.)

I felt embarrassed and ashamed, as if my soul were exposed. The things in my life that had brought me so much joy were in disarray, out of control. The rest of my house was spotless, but hidden away in a closet was a mess. How reflective of my life—the cluttered thoughts, skeletons, and painful memories—while I outwardly appeared so composed.

—*Y. McIntosh, Fairfield, Ohio*

Forgive yourself and bury your skeletons.

Sole Mates

On September 12, 1939, I was just nine years old when Russia invaded my native Poland. The Russians plundered our village and took everything they could carry, including all our shoes. At least they did not take our lowland sheepdog, who was my friend and companion. I could count on his company as I walked to and from school. Since I had no shoes, I walked around barefooted, but this was not an uncommon sight in our village.

Winter was on its way and my parents were concerned that their children were shoeless. Knowing our plight, a neighbor gave me a pair of worn, thigh-high rubber galoshes that he had unearthed from a lakebed. At first they felt heavenly, but they were too large and heavy for my tiny feet. After a few days, my feet developed bruises and blisters that made wearing the galoshes very painful. Since socks were another rare commodity, my mother bandaged my feet with old rags to protect them from bruising and the cold weather. Every day, my mother washed the rags and hung them in front of the fire to dry.

One afternoon on my way home from school, I was down in the dumps about our poor condition and wept as I walked down the familiar path to home. As usual, I spied our dog as he gleefully rushed to accompany me the rest of the way. Bothered by the pain of blisters and the heavy, cumbersome boots, I kicked them off and left them on the snow-covered ground, deciding that it would be more comfortable to walk in the rags that wrapped my feet. After limping for several steps, I turned back around to get those boots. I fell on the cold ground and burst into loud sobs at the sight that met my eyes. Our lowland sheepdog was pushing and pulling and herding my rubber galoshes toward me.

—E. Niedbala, Hadley, Massachusetts

Never give in.
Never give up—Never!

Saving Soles

I do not know when my mother's love for shoes developed, but she had a passion for beautiful, high-quality shoes. She did not own as many shoes as American women, but those she owned were exquisitely crafted by Italians. My parents worked very hard to rebuild after the Russian invasion of Poland and were determined that all four of their children would be successful. My mother cautioned us on a daily basis, "People can take your possessions, but they can never take what's in your head. Get a good education!" Then she would laugh and say, "And don't forget to wear good shoes when you grow up." Bolstered by my parents' experiences, I was determined to succeed and became a registered nurse and midwife. Subsequently, I married a successful tradesman, had two children, and I bought good shoes . . . Italian-made shoes from Giorgio Armani. In our village in Poland, I was known as the woman with the beautiful shoes.

After several years of marriage, my husband and I decided to emigrate to America. The people in our village questioned us about whether we would rent or sell our home. And, of course, the women wanted to know what I was going to do with all my shoes. Just before we left Poland, my husband and I found the poorest family and handed them the keys and papers to our home. In the closet was a gift for the wife . . . all my beautiful shoes.

I can no longer afford to buy shoes by Giorgio Armani for myself, because every month, I buy shoes and send them to my village in Poland for those with no shoes at all.

—E. Niedbala, Hadley, Massachusetts

Pile up the small joys . . .
they'll grow into
mountains of pleasure.

Life is Short, Cherish Your Feet!

Several years ago, while shopping, I noticed a pair of expensive dress heels that were out of my price range. An elegantly dressed older woman standing nearby watched as I ogled them on the display shelf. She had a compelling grace, and a warm smile lit up her face as our eyes met. After picking the display shoe up and then putting it back down, she approached me, and said, "Those shoes are exquisite! Do you like them?"

"Yes," I confided with childlike honesty, "very much so."

"Then try them on!" she said. Before I knew it, I had flagged down a salesperson who asked my size and brought out a pair of the heels from the stockroom. I slipped them on without a thought. Ah, they fit perfectly, like they were made just for me!

"Buy them!" the stranger said with passionate conviction, startling me with the intensity of her command. "I'm seventy-five years old and have finally learned to eat my dessert first. That's how you cut down on your appetite for the stuff you don't really need! First do the things that bring you joy, make you feel good about yourself, and help you to celebrate life. Don't sacrifice your pleasure—buy those shoes!"

I thanked her for sharing her wisdom with me, telling her how much I had needed to hear it. She nodded her head with a short bowing motion, and then disappeared into the crowd. I stared after her for a moment, then bought those shoes. I still have that pair of heels. Every time I wear them, I think of the elegant woman and wonder what life experiences caused her to be so protective of not only her own happiness, but also the happiness of a complete stranger.

—*L. Adams, Albany, Georgia*

*Eat your
dessert first.*

Barefooted Posse

We held a reenactment of my sister's wedding in the States for those family and friends who were unable to attend her destination wedding in Negril, Jamaica. In order to capture the Caribbean spirit, the tables were decorated with bright tropical colors, seashells, sand, and tropical flower garlands. The bridal party wore their original wedding regalia. To everyone's astonishment, one of the bridesmaids walked in barefoot. She forgot her shoes and did not even have a pair of extra dress shoes to wear. Instead of getting upset, the other bridesmaids simply removed their shoes and walked in barefooted. The guests thought it was a novel idea and that our bare feet captured the spirit of the seashores of the Caribbean.

—*M. Mack, Springfield, Massachusetts*

If you make a mountain out of a molehill . . . you will be the only climber.

Shoe Sham!

good friend of mine was vacationing in Arizona and invited me to join her. In passing, I told a colleague of mine about the invitation. She asked if she could join us, since she had never been to that part of the country, and of course lodging was free. I asked my friend and she gladly said yes because we were college roommates and she trusted me. We arrived and had a fantastic time: relaxing, talking, eating at the finest restaurants, and, of course, shopping.

On one of those trips, our hostess found an absolutely eye-catching handbag made of tan leather topped off with a black and tan snakeskin flap. She bought the bag and was determined to find matching shoes. My colleague and I accompanied her, and after two days of hunting, she found the perfect shoes . . . tan and black snakeskin mules with kitten heels. There was only one pair left and it was in her size.

She was elated and I was glad for her. Full of excitement, she showed my colleague her find. My colleague picked up the pair of shoes from the chair where my friend had placed them with another purchase and said, "I want these shoes!" My girlfriend and I laughed. We thought she was joking— but she was not. She walked to the cashier's station and bought the shoes. My friend and I looked at each other, shocked and dumbfounded! This woman was her guest and her visit was not costing her a penny. Furthermore, she still had two days of vacation left. Needless to say, the air in the car could be cut with a knife as we drove home. My friend was a gracious hostess and never said a word. When the end of my colleague's stay arrived, I looked on as she packed away those shoes—along with our friendship.

—*L. Andrews, Los Angeles, California*

In stairways of trust . . .
you have never climbed in vain.

Shoeside Economics

There are four girls in our large family, and we each wear a size eight-and-a-half shoe. My mother limits us to eight pairs per person, but in actuality we each have thirty-two available to wear! It all started when my father built a special hall closet for storing our shoes. Once they were all kept in the same place, my mother came up with the big idea that we should start sharing them with each other. At first we objected to her plan and there was much infighting. But it didn't take much time for us to realize the advantages of having access to four times the numbers of pairs and to come up with a workable agreement. We decided that shoes would be available on a first-come first-served basis, unless one of us had a special engagement and reserved them in advance. The person who buys a new pair always gets to wear them the first time herself before storing them in the common closet. I know it's a somewhat unusual arrangement, but it's taught each of us trust, honesty, sharing, and unconditional love.

—M. Andrews, Ocala, Florida

Share and you shall multiply.

Lost Sole

Everyone laughed when I told them I lost one shoe on a night out with the girls. "It could only have happened to you!" and "It must have been a hell of a night!" were the replies. I did not know where or when I lost my shoe, or even that it was missing until I was ready to wear them again. I guess I hobbled around with one shoe—it must have been a funny sight to all those who noticed. I too thought it was funny at first, but I stopped laughing when I realized that this incident reflected my careless attitudes of the past—it really hit home! I have been negligent and careless with my life, my talents, my words, my friends, and my opportunities. I am not laughing now.

—C. Cooke, West Orange, New Jersey

Be good to yourself . . . we teach people how to treat us.

Soldier On, Ferragamo

As a young engineer, I was given my first field assignment. I had recently joined a firm in Cincinnati and was asked to assist a more seasoned engineer at a new plant being built in Georgia. Arriving at the construction site, and wanting to impress my employers on my first day, I had on impressive business attire, including a pair of expensive Ferragamo shoes. After meeting with the senior engineer in the program office, he asked me to accompany him on a tour of the facilities. After touring the building, he took me outside to visit the plant utility site. As we approached the building, we confronted a large field of red, muddy clay. Turning toward me, the senior engineer halted long enough to glance at my feet and then said, "Come on, follow me!" Off into the mud we went.

—W. Williams, Albany, Georgia

Don't be afraid of the dirty work.

Mind Your Own Shoe

It was the end of the day and I was exhausted from searching for the perfect pair of shoes to wear for an upcoming evening affair. I love shoes, and I don't buy just any type, only the best—the ones that talk to you. They have to be really unique. I decided to try one more store and saw a couple of pairs that had possibilities. While waiting for the salesperson to bring them out for me, and just as I was getting ready to plop myself down in the nearest chair, I spied a gorgeous pair on the floor next to a shoebox. I leapt across the room to grab them before anyone else could. *They're the perfect style to match my outfit and exactly my size,* I thought to myself after pushing my stocking feet into them. I was getting up to take them to the cash register when a voice from behind me belted out, "Lady, those are my shoes. I bought them in Italy last year!"

—C. Andrews, Atlanta, Georgia

Look before
you leap.

Life is a trip—
catch yourself.

On Point at Work

This shoe memory is as clear to me today as when it happened twenty-five years ago. I was fresh out of college and had landed a job as receptionist at a New York City advertising agency. On my first day, dressed to the nines and with briefcase in hand, I got off the elevator and strutted down the narrow hallway to the door of the agency. Suddenly, I felt like the floor had been pulled out from under me. As I stumbled forward, grasping at the walls to catch my fall, out of the corner of my eye I saw something ricocheting off the walls, tumbling down the hallway. It came to a rest square in front of the agency door. Limping and horrified, I realized it was the right heel of my expensive bone-colored Etienne Aigner pumps that I had bought the day before! I made my grand entry into the corporate world hobbling on one leg with heel in hand. Some first impression! For the rest of the day, I wore my commuting shoes—a pair of flat, beat-up brown Docksiders from my college days—with my beautiful pink corporate suit.

—J. Bianco, Manhattan, NY

The Sole I Gave Away

*I*t was a must-have purchase and it didn't matter that nothing in my closet matched the fabulous pair of dress shoes I impulsively bought. Even though I had nowhere to wear them, at least once a month I would take them out of the closet, put them on, and admire them in the mirror. I knew they were one of my best shoe purchases ever!

About a year later, my sister paid me a weekend visit. After I paraded my prized shoes in front of her, she told me she had something perfect to wear with them and asked if I would give them to her. I told her, "No way!" But on the day of my sister's departure, I opened her suitcase and put the shoes inside. You cannot imagine her joy when she returned home to discover my unexpected gift. Several months later, I lost my sister. She was buried with those shoes on her feet.

—*Y. Sun, Belmont, Trinidad*

Have no regrets.

All God's Children Got Shoes

I sat on the wooden pew next to Big Mamma in church on Sundays, the air infused with the music of spirituals. The rhythmic answering, shouts, refrains, hand clapping, foot stomping, and deep baritone and bass voices gave me goosebumps. The voices of tenors and sopranos made me want to sing even louder. There was no need for a piano, which our church could not afford—we made our own sweet music. One of Big Mamma's favorite spirituals started with "I got a song, you got a song" progressing to "I got a harp, a robe, wings," and finally on to "I got shoes, you got shoes, all God's children got shoes. When I get to heaven I'm gonna put on my shoes, I'm gonna walk all over God's heaven, heaven, heaven."

My voice was always silent when they sang the part about "I got shoes" because I didn't have any—at least, not ones that were bought just for me. We were dirt poor and I wore used, beaten-up, hand-me-down shoes—other people's shoes. I was God's child, but I didn't have my own shoes. How could I walk all over God's heaven? Big Mamma would say,

"Sing, child!" but I kept my voice quiet, vowing not to sing those words until I knew what it was like to own and walk in my own shoes. That childhood yearning inspired me to become very accomplished later in life. I can now buy any shoes that I desire, and walk in them anywhere I want to go. And this, to me, is heaven!

—*E. Mitchell, Los Angeles, California*

*The best shoes
are heaven-sent.*

From City Pumps
to Bass Boots

My favorite shoes are a pair of Bass mountain boots, which I bought more than six years ago when I put away my city pumps and moved to the country to start a public relations business out of my home. They are beautiful, light brown leather with a woven tassel on the side. Casually stylish, they are flat and comfy even with a pair of heavy socks. I wear them year-round while tromping through the mud and in our fields. Although they are now worn and stained from use, these boots remind me of my transition from the city to the country, and from having a boss to working for myself. They have become symbols of what I love most about my new life: watching the seasons change, hiking through the woods, working in my garden, and being able to wear whatever I want to work. As the reputation of my company has grown, I've finally worked up the courage to keep on my Bass boots, even when my clients come for meetings.

—J. Rhoman, Blandford, Massachusetts

Be a trailblazer!

Thigh-High Therapy

My much-older cousin told me that roughly ten years ago rumors were flying that her husband was having an affair. She had no proof, but began to search through his belongings for evidence. During one of those searches, she uncovered an envelope with another woman's name written on it neatly tucked away under the driver's seat of his car. She opened it and found five one-hundred-dollar bills. Although hurt and disappointed, she took the money and returned the envelope to exactly where she found it, never mentioning a word to her husband. The next day, my cousin went out and bought a pair of black, thigh-high leather boots costing exactly $500. The rumors abruptly stopped, and they've been uneventfully married ever since.

—U. Andrews, Queens, New York

Sometimes you can say everything with a pair of shoes.

The Bunionectomy Conundrum

Both my mother and grandmother developed bunions that made wearing regular shoes unbearably painful for them. I grew up watching Mom cut holes in the leather to make room for her bunions and being grossed out by Grandma's special black numbers—orthopedic clodhoppers that were attractive only if you lived in a convent. Grandma Anna had come right off the boat from Sicily, where worn feet were part and parcel of other agrarian traits—hardworking calloused hands, skin weathered by the sun, and ample padding around hips and thighs.

I hoped the foot curse would skip a generation, but it didn't. So when the early-warning signs of bunions appeared—and not wanting to cut holes in my shoes or give in to a life of ugly footwear—I opted for painful bunionectomy surgery, hoping for those sleek and sexy feet I so admired. But to my dismay, instead I ended up with a second toe longer than the first and the same un-sexy shoe collection as before.

Finally, a friend suggested that I accept my ugly feet by "accessorizing." As I sit here today, they are adorned with red polish, champagne-glass decals, and a variety of exotic toe rings. I now take pride in my feet—and they've become a good topic of conversation during open-toe season. I think Grandma Anna would approve.

—*L. Foggini, San Francisco, California*

Work with what you've got.

Shoe Divas Unite!

A pair of espadrilles brought one of my dearest friends into my life. For two-and-a-half years, I noticed the large Potomac Mills sign we drove by each time we visited our daughter at the College of William and Mary in Williamsburg, Virginia. My husband said that it was probably an old cotton mill. But my curiosity persisted, and next time we were in the area, I asked about Potomac Mills. I almost hyperventilated upon hearing that it was the largest retail outlet center on the East Coast! So at the end of that school year, after picking up my daughter to bring her home for the summer, we stopped at the outlet center to do a little shopping.

My daughter was trying on a pair of espadrilles when a charming woman complimented her on the shoes she had chosen. The woman introduced herself to us. It turned out that her daughter also attended William and Mary. Although we had many things in common (including our passion for shoes), over the years we've learned to lovingly accept our differences: religion, ethnicity, and political beliefs. Our friendship has been broken in and has grown comfortable like a pair of old shoes. Though not in agreement at all times, we always find understanding from each other. And while others have put on their shoes and walked out of our lives, we continue to take ours off and stay.

—C. Riccio, Elverson, Pennsylvania

There are no chance meetings in life.

A Saving Grace
for Aching Feet

My aunt is always inviting me to church. Every time I see her, she says, "Baby, see you in church." And I respond, "Did someone die?" or "Who's getting married?" Not too long ago she invited me to the annual church picnic. She was surprised—in fact, shocked—when I said yes.

I arrived at the picnic with sensual red lips and wearing my attract-a-husband outfit: tight jeans and Delilah animal-print leather high heels. I was ready to eat and then hunt for a husband. Shortly after I got there, my feet began to ache and I noticed they were swollen. After an hour or so the pain intensified so much so that I found it difficult to walk in those tight, high-heeled shoes.

Bracing against the pain, I struggled to the food line and while there, I couldn't help but share my discomfort with one of the church sisters. The stranger took off her comfortable sassy shoes, saying, "Here, wear mine, I'll wear yours." As I walked back to my table in her comfy shoes, tears filled my eyes. Not only was I overwhelmed by this stranger's kindness, but it struck me that all my life, I had been looking for love in all the wrong places.

—W. Burns, Winston-Salem, North Carolina

Love is the essence of life . . .
sprinkle a few drops.

Irish Soles

My parents loved America, but their hearts belonged to their native Ireland. We were surrounded by Irish immigrants in our adopted country and our home reflected many Irish traditions, down to the humor, drink, and dance. Therefore, when my sister and I became of age, step dancing was not a choice, but a requirement. As I gleefully encountered neighborhood friends in passing, we would greet each other and ask, "Where do you take?" We never finished the sentence with " . . . Irish dancing?" We all knew what "where do you take?" meant.

I started dancing in soft shoes, which were much more forgiving of mistakes than traditional tap shoes. The "naturals" moved quickly to tap shoes. Oh, the joy of being

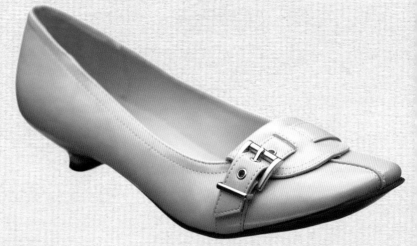

promoted to "taps." What ecstatic sounds! The thunderous battering of hard shoes on wooden stages was not only music to my ears, but the sound of pride and accomplishment. Every beat was heard, every mistake obvious, and along with the glory came the pressure. During St. Patrick's Day celebrations, dancers were given the opportunity to perform at the many functions held in honor of the Irish holiday. Everyone waited with bated breath to see who would be chosen to dance in those priceless tap shoes. There was joyous celebration for those chosen to represent their school of dance, and heartache for those left behind.

Going from soft shoes to tap shoes is reminiscent of the real world—lessons are learned in many arenas and stages— some are easy and forgiving, while others are hard and unforgiving.

—*E. Murphy, Wilbraham, Massachusetts*

One step starts your journey.

Finding Your Pace

I have lived a very long life and have worn many shoes during my lifetime. But now I own only a few pairs that are practical and serve specific functions. Out of these, I find myself attached to a pair of black loafers that I have worn for the last ten years. These shoes are well crafted and made to last; the leather is soft, is of high quality, and has formed to my feet. Although the soles and heels have been replaced, and the scuffs have been restained and repolished, they have withstood the test of time. These shoes are strong, reliable, and safe—they have walked me through sunshine and shade and have what I call an unassuming personality. These loafers remind me of the bonds and qualities of friendship, and that friendship takes years to build and also withstands the test of time. Like my shoes, it is the comfort of feeling safe with those I trust and have opened my heart to. As I repaired my shoes, it made me understand the importance of repairing and rebuilding relationships. I have learned that we have to treat our friends well to keep them because, like my shoes, good friends are irreplaceable.

—P. Williams, Manhattan Beach, California

Good friends repair and cherish.

Death of My Shoe

I was born in Barbour County, Alabama, in Eufaula, a small town located on the southeastern border of the state. We small-town kids did not have the luxury of traveling the three miles to school on school busses, so we took the quickest way—through the woods and across the railroad tracks. One day, I was walking home from school on the train tracks when we heard the sound of the train's whistle in the distance. We began to scamper off the tracks, but my laced-up shoe got caught in the tracks where a spur line joined the main rail. I fell on the tracks and let out a scream for fear that I was going to be run over by the oncoming train. My cousin tried pulling me out by the arms, then by my leg, but my shoe did not budge. It seemed like a lifetime! The train's whistle blew in loud successions, warning of its approach. I knew it was the end. Suddenly my cousin began to feverishly unlace my shoe. I pulled my foot out, leaving my shoe wedged in the tracks, and ran for my life.

—V. Adams, Jersey City, New Jersey

Sometimes what we're forced to leave behind wasn't meant to follow us through life.

Center Stage

I arrived at the function arm in arm with my fiancé and dressed to the nines: short, champagne-colored chiffon cocktail dress, sapphire and pearl chandelier earrings, and a pair of scandalous Jimmy Choos that accentuated my ankles and legs. I looked so good I could not stand myself! As I greeted acquaintances and friends I scanned the crowd for my fiancé's ex-girlfriend. I knew that she was going to be there, and I wanted to show her what he now had. After zooming in on her, I slowly strutted in her direction. I was so taken with myself and intent on showing off my stuff to the ex, I did not pay attention to where I was walking. The heel of my shoes got caught in the fringe of the Persian rug that graced the floor and I fell face down in front of everyone.

—*V. Rossi, Long Island, New York*

It is not falling down but getting up that makes you stronger.

On the Run

I am always late, in a hurry, and cannot find the shoes I want to wear in my closet full of too small, too old, too ugly, too out-of-style, too high, too loud, too sexy, too tight shoes. Each time I cannot find the ones that I need, I settle and wear a pair of shoes that I had not planned on wearing and really don't want to wear. Whenever this happens, I promise myself that I will go through my piles of shoes and throw out the ones I don't need or want. But I never do. I keep them all. Then, again and again, I go through the cycle of frustration I've created.

—M. Hanson, Danbury, Connecticut

Get off the merry-go-round and recover your balance!

Try This One On for Size!

While vacationing in England, I spied a pair of shoes in the window of Shelly's of London: they were navy blue mules, with three-inch navy heels and a contrasting light blue stripe. I wanted a pair, but the largest size they carried was nine and I needed a nine and a half. Although my heels hung over the edge of the back of the shoes, the assistant encouraged me to buy them because they looked good on my feet. I was reluctant, but gave in and bought the size nine. I could only wear them with long pants that covered my heels. Even though I knew the shoes were too small and would never fit properly, I continued to hold on to them, trying to press my feet further into them. Finally I became constrained by these striking shoes, so I gave them away. It is very much like life: sometimes we are encouraged to settle for less, for the things we do not need or want.

—D.L. Williams, Wilbraham, Massachusetts

When in doubt, say "No."

Short Lived

I was thirteen years old and everyone at school was wearing penny loafers with brand-new pennies stuck in the front. Students would hoard shiny new pennies so they could replace dull ones. I wanted a pair of penny loafers badly, so I asked my mother to buy me a pair. She did not have the money then and there, but she took me to the store so I could try some on and get the perfect fit. My heart skipped a beat when I saw those shoes on my feet.

Then the day arrived. It was a glorious Saturday morning. My mother had to work, so she gave me the money to buy those penny loafers. I bought the shoes and tightly clutched them as I boarded the bus for the short ride home. When the bus reached my stop, I excitedly jumped up and ran off the bus, eager to show off my new shoes to my friends. As the bus pulled off, I realized that I had left my shoes on the bus. The scene is quite vivid in my mind: I can still see myself running after the bus as it drove away with my brand new pair of penny loafers.

—M. Martin, Springfield, Massachusetts

Hold on to what you have.

Who Gets the House, Who Gets the Chukkas?

During the 1970s, while in my early twenties, I married a man who had the same sized feet as mine. Those were the unisex fashion years, so we were able to share some of the same shoes. Our mutual favorite was a pair of tan, suede chukka boots. During the winter, we alternated days of wearing them. Unfortunately, as with many youthful marriages, ours did not make it past the five-year mark. When it came time to separate, we were able to quickly agree on who got the apartment, the stereo, the couch, the Persian rug given to us by friends as a wedding present, and even the dog. But no matter how hard we tried, we could not agree on custody of the cherished chukka boots. Finally, a mutual friend mediated. The solution? We donated them to the local Goodwill store. The shoes were gone, the fighting stopped, and we were able to divorce in peace.

—M. Meyer, Santa Barbara, California

Peace is achieved when we still the storms of our minds.

"Shhh . . . New Shoes"

While enjoying a glass of wine, soft music, and, I am sure, a moment of insanity, I agreed with my husband that I had too many shoes and did not need to buy another pair for a while. At that moment of psychosis I am sure I meant to keep the promise, but every woman knows that giving up new shoes is akin to giving up air. It was early March, three months after my commitment. My spring shoes were still in the attic and I was suffering from spring fever when I took an unexpected trip to Copley Plaza in Boston. After about an hour or so of window shopping, I walked right into the shoe department of Neiman Marcus, tried on what caught my eye, and without thinking, bought a stunning pair of bone-colored, high-heeled slides that went well with the outfit I was going to wear to dinner that night with my husband and friends.

I left the store, locked my purchase in the trunk, drove home, parked the car, and went inside to see if my husband had beaten me home. He was not there. I breathed a sigh of relief, then hurried to the car, retrieved my new shoes, scurried inside, and took them right up to the attic and mixed them in with my other shoes. Before getting dressed for dinner, I went to the attic and brought down my shoes for the season, then asked my husband what went with the outfit I had laid out to wear. Of course he did not choose the right pair, which were the new ones, but I did. At dinner, everyone—including the men—complimented me on my shoes and wanted to know if they were a recent purchase. My husband said, "No, they were in the attic," but we girls winked. We knew the truth.

—J. Gregory, Peabody, Massachusetts

Don't make impossible promises!

Slipping Out of Character

After graduating from college, I was employed as a buyer of clothes and shoes, and at one point in my career, I owned 145 pairs. One day I was off to see my doctor adorned in a new pair of pink leather thong slippers with flowers. My physician fell in love with my shoes as soon as she saw them. I asked her what size shoe she wore. She said size seven, which was the size of my shoes. Imagine her surprise when I took off my slippers, gave them to her, and walked out her office barefooted.

—*N. Mozdzanowski,*
Agawam, Massachusetts

Surprises take the dreariness out of life.

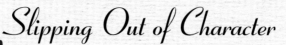

Life is nothing without comfort!

My Old Shoes

I have had my favorite pair of shoes for ages. I must have bought these shoes about ten years ago. They are just like old friends. I have worked these shoes in until they have formed to my feet. My friends have a soft inset and firm leather that never falls apart, even after years of stress. I wear heels all week long, but on Friday, I pull out my old shoes and my feet feel a welcome release. Sometimes I get so busy, I forget that they are there for me. But when I remember, I just think of the comfort my feet are going to feel. I can always find them—in the bottom of my closet, on the back porch, or even at the edge of my bed. I will never give them up and I'll never find a pair like them again.

—T. Benton Whitley, Springfield, Massachusetts

My Shoe Angel

My husband and I were on our way from upstate New York to my job interview that was three hours away. As planned, we stopped at the last rest area so I could change my clothes and present a fresh and professional look to my prospective employers. After freshening up and slipping on my professional attire, we got back into the car and headed on our way with excitement. We had driven about forty-five minutes when I noticed that I was still wearing slippers. Not only that, I had forgotten my dress shoes at the rest stop. We considered backtracking, but we did not have the hour-and-a-half it would take and there was a strong possibility my shoes would not be there.

All sorts of excuses flooded my mind. Could I tell the human resources personnel I had a temporary foot condition that required my wearing slippers? I could go in there limping and tell them I had sprained my ankle or broken my toe. Perhaps I could wear my husband's loafers. Dress shoes or not, I was determined to make that interview and get that position.

We arrived at our destination with thirty minutes to spare, so we prayerfully drove around to see if we could find a place for me to buy shoes, even though it was eight o'clock in the morning. Fortunately for me, I found a little shoe shop and was able to buy a pair of shoes. And I got the position.

—D. Robinson, Springfield, Massachusetts

Don't make
an irritation
into a
misfortune.

Throw Out the Shoes

I walked into my favorite shoe repair shop and observed a discussion between the Portuguese owner and a woman who was holding a pair of white satin, high-heeled pumps that looked as if they had seen one too many parties. She was trying to convince this expert cobbler to dye the shoes for her. I think he said no in every language he knew and it was quite obvious that he was not going to be coerced into dying the indelibly stained shoes. After many repeated refusals, the frustrated shoe repairman said, "Lady, I'll give you a new sole, I will even heel for you, but I will not dye for you."

—*V. Robinson, Springfield, Massachusetts*

*Understand . . .
some things aren't
worth saving.*

Free Spirit

"You are what?!" is the response I get when people find out that I am a female rock climber. And women, more so than men, are aghast when I tell them that my rock climbing shoes are two sizes smaller than my regular shoe size. The conversation always regresses to the pain and difficulty of wearing tight shoes. But to me, rock climbing is a perpendicular chess game, a vertical ballet that is conducted in high performance slippers. Although tight, they are not so tight that my circulation is cut off. My shoes fit properly and comfortably and provide the grip power that handles small rock pockets and thick edges with superiority. I can feel the edge of a dime with my tight shoes!

—L. O'Brien, Washington, D.C.

Set goals and climb heights in your own shoes.

Soaring on Shoes
with Wings

For years I worked for a controlling boss who sought to govern my every move, even while I was not at work. It was like wearing tight shoes every single day. I felt that I had to stick it out because I was a newly divorced, single mom trying to make ends meet; the pay was good and I had a unique opportunity to develop my talents. Sundays were nightmares because Mondays were the beginning of the work week and I had to shove my feet in those unspeakably tight shoes that caused corns on my feet, burns on my heart, upset stomach, and headaches. I was being squeezed to death from my feet on up when I decided that I had to kick off those tight shoes. I formed a business, turned in my resignation, and left. Now I am soaring on shoes with wings.

—*A. Hennessey, Wilbraham, Massachusetts*

Take control of your destiny
. . . never creep when
you can soar.

My Own Shoe Story

A place for you to capture your own shoe story.

Tips on Hosting a Shoe Party

Sole Purpose

Shoe Parties ignite excitement from the moment the invitation arrives until the party dust settles. They are filled with wonderful reasons for friends to get together and have fun while celebrating their lives through humorous or poignant shoe stories. And a shoe party provides a marvelous opportunity for each woman to symbolically throw out something that causes her pain as she discards shoes that are too tight.

Strutting with Style: Setting the Mood

Compile a guest list of friends who enjoy each other's company and are willing to participate in the ritual of sharing through storytelling. Create a warm and inviting environment with scrumptious refreshments, mellow music, and soothing beverages.

Ask your guests to:

- wear their favorite shoes
- bring a pair of tight shoes or a pair of new shoes to donate to charity and
- bring their favorite desserts for sharing

Sole to Soul:
Where Have Your Soles Taken You?

Have each woman introduce herself and show off her favorite shoe. Give her an opportunity to briefly share with the group why the shoes she's worn are her favorite. It's now shoe story time! Here your guests tell their humorous or poignant shoe stories and the lessons learned.

Walking on Ceremony

Have your guests form a circle while holding the tight shoes they brought with them. Ask guests to think of something in their lives that causes them pain that they are willing to release. This liberating ritual gives each woman an opportunity to come to terms quietly with something that hurts. As the decision is made, each woman takes a turn, walks to the center of the circle, and discards her pair of tight shoes that symbolizes the discomfort and pain she is giving up, never to take on again.

Make memories worth remembering!

About the Author

Yvonne L. Williams, M.Ed., inspirational speaker and author, is a native of Trinidad, West Indies, and migrated to her adopted country, the U.S., some thirty years ago. She has been victorious over three simultaneous primary cancers located in four areas and believes that a day with tight shoes is still a wonderful day. She is married to William, is the mother of two, and grandmother of Kasen Jeffrey and Gabrielle La Rea.